Osgood Eaton Fuller

The Year of Christ in Song

Advent and Christmastide. Second Edition

Osgood Eaton Fuller

The Year of Christ in Song
Advent and Christmastide. Second Edition

ISBN/EAN: 9783337379711

Printed in Europe, USA, Canada, Australia, Japan

Cover: Foto ©Thomas Meinert / pixelio.de

More available books at **www.hansebooks.com**

The Year of Christ

In Song.

Advent and Christmas-Tide.

BY
OSGOOD E. FULLER, A. M.,

RECTOR OF THE CHURCH OF THE MESSIAH, LINDEN,
AND LATE MASTER OF LATIMER HALL, FENTON.

SECOND THOUSAND.

DETROIT:
FRED. G. GIBBS,
181 WOODWARD AVENUE.
1876.

Entered according to Act of Congress, in the Year 1875, by
OSGOOD E. FULLER,
In the Office of the Librarian of Congress at Washington.

EMIL SCHOBER, PRINTER,
DETROIT.

E. B. SMITH & CO., BINDERS,
DETROIT.

Preface.

The Church has in every age furnished Poets, Sculptors and Painters with their sublimest subjects. And, like Nature, Catholic and prodigal in all her hidden stores, she still possesses inexhaustable veins of Poesy and Art, that have hardly been touched. Yet the taste of the age discourages those who have a heart to work them, by either hugging the delusion that the best of God's precious ores have all been mined, or showing an almost exclusive fondness for ephemeral themes. This book tries to breast the current.

None of the Poems contained in this volume have been written from a purely literary stand-point; and very few of them, for the place they here occupy. They are, for the most part, the natural out-growth of a pastoral and educational work extending through a considerable number of years. The Author has endeavored to project into them all something of Christian experience — an experience in which he recognized the fashioning Hand of Providence as well in the cloud as in the sunshine of life. For all this he believes they will prove the more profitable to the thoughtful reader.

The Year of Christ, like the firmament, is set with many lights, one, indeed, exceeding another in glory, but all of unspeakable value to the pilgrim who is seeking the Celestial Country. It has been the Author's aim not only to offer here and there a spiritual song, suggested by the splendor of the way, but often to present a poem of greater length, as the sublimity of the season, or the things of his own life, inspired.

The second poem, "The Light of the Virgin, or, Pursuit of the Ideal," was composed just before the writer was formally enrolled with the people of God. He thinks it is rightly placed on the threshold of the Christian Year.

Advent, 1875.

Contents.

	Page
The Year of Christ	7
Lux Virginis, or Pursuit of the Ideal	21
The Kingdom of God	27
Into His Chambers	30
The Beautiful Plant	33
Eureka	37
The Triumphal Entry	48
The Eternal Song	49
Signs	57
Ordination Hymns	58
The Day of God	60
Angels of Life and Death	61
The Doubters' Hymn	67
A Legend of St Thomas	68

	Page
Epithalamium	72
Advent Longing	84
The Nativity	85
The Christmas Service	89
A Christmas Carol, with Music	98
The Death of St. Stephen, with Music	102
A Legend of St. John	106
The Holy Innocents	113
Ecclesia	119
Engagement Song	121
The Marriage Garment	122
The Traveler	124
New Year Day	130

THE YEAR OF CHRIST.

PROLOGUE.

"How beautiful upon the mountains."

Tune, *Wir Pflugen*.   See page 102.

I.

How fair upon the mountains
Where beauty shall not cease,
The feet that bring good tidings,
The lips that publish peace!
In all the dreams of boyhood
That beauty had control,
And now those years have vanished,
It has not left my soul.

For when I hear the Gospel
From some great heart out told,
With tharks for those good tidings
That will not aye grow old,
The beauty on the mountains,
Whose vision shall not cease,
Within my heart upflashes
With all the olden peace.

II.

On mountains in the circle
Of many a year of Christ,
I tracked His life undying,
And felt a joy unpriced —
The joy that is forever
To one dear purpose born,
As morning unto evening,
And evening unto morn.

PROLOGUE.

And in the hope of heaven
Whose beauty bends to earth,
I sought, as unto sunshine,
To grow toward His worth,
What time in grace that cometh
From one eternal source,
I drank the cup of nurture
And held me on my course.

It was His love undying
In which alone I stood,
And here and there accomplished
The little that I could.
And unto Christ be glory,
If, with His sandals shod,
I rescue from the desert
Another child of God.

III.

Not all of earth is earthy,
Nor all beyond sublime:
Eternity hath sorrow,
And joy is found in time.
And joy is everlasting,
A thing heroic, born
Of doing and pursuing
In regions of the morn,

Whate'er the Spirit willeth,
Which hath of souls the cure,
Whate'er a soul becometh
That must for aye endure;
Through evil fame and happy,
Until the setting sun
Proclaims in dying beauty
The race of earth is run.

And what if darkness gathers,
Which is not darkness all?
And what if sorrows thicken,
Which cannot hold in thrall?
Oh think ye not of darkness
Where blessed light abides.
Oh think ye not of sorrow
Where deathless joy resides.

The days so few and evil,
That dawn on mortal eyes,
Reveal the blessed mountains
Whose beauty never dies;
The dear and blessed mountains
Which longing eyes behold,
Begirt with all that lureth
The eager heart and bold.

Oh who would not ascend them
And cool the fever heat,
The burning pain and ceasless,
Which in his being meet,

And all the sweet pulsation
Of manly triumph feel,
As ever upward pressing
With pilgrim faith and zeal?

In grand and twilight glory
Like hoary priests they stand
And drop their benedictions
Upon a toiling land;
What time they seem to beckon
To those who dwell below,
Revealing and concealing
What mortals pine to know:

Concealing what of knowledge
Might quench and satisfy
The mighty thirst and hunger
Which bridge the earth and sky:
Revealing as in mercy
A prospect here and there,
Majestically real
And infinitely fair;

PROLOGUE.

And flaming down the watchword
Of all the good to be,
On those who look above them
With eager eyes to see,
Which, writ upon their banner
In characters of fire,
Out shines the blaze of passion
And every low desire;

Until, like him who scenteth
Some far off golden shore,
And girdeth for the journey,
Not counting dangers o'er,
New purposed, bold and eager,
They put their armor on,
Intent those heights in reaching
From whence the light has shone;

While ever, as ascending,
They feed the flame of life
And nurse a nobler purpose
And nerve for bolder strife,

Till on the blessed mountains
They raise the victor's cry,
And rest, begirt with glory
Which cannot fade or die.

And rest? There is no resting,
No one abiding place
For mortals or immortals
In life's unending race:
The grave it doth not limit
The strong heroic will:
Fair fields and everlasting
Invite endeavor still.

For joy goes on, forever
To one dear purpose born,
As morning unto evening
And evening unto morn.
And mountains rise on mountains
Which touch remoter skies,
And bless with larger blessing
The soul that never dies.

Oh who would not ascend them,
The table lands of God,
By earth and heaven's heroes
Victoriously trod ;
Where rest is found in action,
And joy in ceaseless love,
Which hath below beginning
And waxeth strong above!

IV.

WHAT time an eager pilgrim
For many a year was I,
The beauty on the mountains
Did fill my wistful eye;
For all within the circle
Of each new year of Christ,
I tracked His life undying
And felt a joy unpriced.

Sometimes a form of beauty,
Sometimes a hidden law,
One vision went before me
And held the mind in awe
And oh, I could not linger,
Though sunk in half despair;
For what I ever followed,
Did ever grow more fair.

Forever some new glory,
Behind the clouds in part,
Did wrap the soul in wonder
And feed the hungry heart.
The light relieved the darkness,
The darkness dimmed the light,
And half in light and shadow
I went from height to height.

Sometimes I rose in falling,
Sometimes in rising fell,
And all the sweet and bitter
I cannot pause to tell.

PROLOGUE.

But conquest came forever,
As gladness after pain;
And who would scorn the anguish,
To follow in her train?

For all within the circle
Of many a year of Christ,
I tracked His life undying
And felt a joy unpriced,—
The joy that is forever
To one dear purpose born,
As morning unto evening
And evening unto morn.

And all I gained and gathered
I hid within my heart,
Where year by year it groweth
Of this poor life a part;
Till now my only purpose
Is how I best may guide
Some weary, toiling brother
Far up the mountain side.

Oh, if I aught have garnered
Of life's bright, golden grain,
It is my dear ambition
To sow it all again.
And God I know will help me
And give me inward peace,
And thus for all my sowing
My little store increase.

Advent

and

Christmas-tide.

(FIRST SERIES.)

TO

HENRY P. TAPPAN, D. D., LL. D.,

THE CHIEF ORGANIZER
OF THE UNIVERSITY OF MICHIGAN,
THE GREAT CHANCELLOR OF THE SAME
FOR TWELVE YEARS,
WHOSE HOME IS NOW IN A FOREIGN LAND,
TO WHOM THE AUTHOR IS LARGELY INDEBTED
FOR WHATEVER DEVOTION HE HAS SHOWN
TO A BEAUTIFUL AND LOFTY IDEAL,
THE INITIAL POEM
OF THIS ADVENT AND CHRISTMAS-TIDE SERIES
IS, WITHOUT HIS KNOWLEDGE,
AFFECTIONATELY AND REVERENTLY
INSCRIBED
BY HIS GRATEFUL
PUPIL.

LUX VIRGINIS;

OR,

PURSUIT OF THE IDEAL.

"Fair as the moon, clear as the sun, and terrible as an army with banners."

I ADORE an airy maiden,
   And I bless her night and day:
Night and day where'er I wander,
   She is ever on my way.

Tender maiden, watchful maiden,
   Friend to me she is alway,
And with countenance angelic
   All my baser thoughts doth fray.

Now she chides me and she guides me,
   If by chance I go astray:
Then she scorns me and she warns me,
   If to rest my head I lay.

Purer than the virgin dew-drops,
  And more beautiful than they,
Clothed she is in lily-meekness
  And a youth forever May.

Who would not rejoice to woo her,
  Who is clad in such array?
Who would not rejoice to win her,
  Who may never know decay?

Fairer maiden, rarer maiden,
  Poet never may portray;
Purer maiden, truer maiden,
  Never dwelt in mortal clay.

And such charms she always weareth,
  And so modest to display!
Oh my airy, fairy maiden
  Over me hath perfect sway!

Should King Oberon, the Fairy,
  Haply from his kingdom stray,
And be questioned if he love her,
  He could never answer nay;

Such his eager heart to woo her,
    And her to his realm convey,
Where her beauty would enthrone her
    Queen of every elf and fay.

Oh, her smile to me is better
    Than the vintage of Tokay;
Better hours when I behold her
    Than are ages of Cathay.

But, ah me! she e'er so coy is —
    And I always hate delay —
Oft my heart grows dark within me,
    Void of hope's celestial ray.

For when I would fain embrace her,
    Blushingly she flits away,
Darting, glancing like a sunbeam,
    As if mocking my dismay;

Leaving me, and then returning,
    Like the sunlight in the spray;
And my soul is half distracted
    With such Tantalus-survey.

Why will not the cruel maiden
  Once my beauty-thirst allay?
Doth she stoop at last to vengeance,
  Dooming me a castaway?

Airy maiden, fairy maiden,
  Do not keep me thus at bay;
Linger yet a little, maiden;
  Maiden, yet a little stay.

Ah, she will not deign to listen,
 . Though I sue and I inveigh;
Ah, she will not deign to listen,
  Doth she then my love repay?

If I ask her if she love me,
  Blushing she will nothing say,
Nothing answer to convince me,
  Nothing, neither nay nor yea.

But retreating, softly fleeting,
  Like a rainbow heavenly gay,
She doth call me, she doth call me,
  And I cannot but obey.

And as bold and eager-hearted
  As a school-boy who at play,
Bright-hued butterflies in chasing
  O'er the fragrant, new mown hay,

Vexed, successless, yet determined
  On the capture of his prey,
Which allures him and eludes him,
  Follow softly as he may;

I pursue my airy maiden
  From the morning twilight grey,
Till the mists of evening gather,
  And no conquest doth defray

All my yearnings and my heart-beats,
  For she every art doth slay.
Yet with new and light endeavor,
  To allure her I essay,

Purposing no base inaction
  And no sluggard's welaway,
Till I touch the happy altar,
  Crowned on with the fadeless bay.

And I think my heart grows better,
    And I count not what I pay
For the airy chase and earthly,
    Where she seemeth to betray;

For I feel if here I never
    Win my maiden, as I pray,
I shall in yon sphere eternal
    Fold her in my arms for aye;

Where the splendor of the virgin
    Satisfies the heart straightway,
And the rhyme that never changes,
    Fringes the Celestial Lay.

The Kingdom of God.

Awake, O dreamers, rejoice, rejoice!
  For the Kingdom of God is at hand,
And the call of the beautiful maiden's voice
  Is blending with manhood's command.

The vision of fair and holy things
  Will never conquer the world,
Without the faith which to heaven flings
  The banner too brave to be furled.

In the shadowy field, where the battle is set,
  Put on the armor of light,
And know ye the foes, who with valor are met,
  Shall vanish with the night.

The day is at hand, and the wilderness
  Echoes, Repent! repent!
And show ye the beauty of holiness
  In doing the Lord's intent.

And the manly voice of the hermit, John,
  Is the voice of Christ in the land:
Repent!—all ages shall bear it on—
  For the Kingdom of God is at hand

II.

The years are big with the things of fate,
  The ages are piled with gold—
For the gold of God is it too late,
  The world is so very old?

And men are starving, though bountiful store
  Is offered through all the land,
Not heeding the cry for evermore,
  The Kingdom of God is at hand.

THE KINGDOM OF GOD.

The bread of God is just as sweet
   As it was in the olden time,
And the hungry hearts, that freely eat,
   Shall grow to a life sublime.

Alas, that Famine and Hate are abroad
   And Wrong is a king with men,
When day and night are prayers to the Lord
   For Mercy and Right again!

But men must suffer, and men must pray,
   And the valiant saints strike home,
Until the cry of the Advent Day,
   The Kingdom of God is come.

INTO HIS CHAMBERS.

"Thy love is better than wine."

I APPROACHED the lordly chambers,
  Which arose at God's command,
More majestic than all temples,
  Poets find in fairy land.

I approached the lofty chambers,
  Which for man are filled with good,
And with awe and fear upon me
  At the sacred threshold stood.

"Oh for strength! and oh for courage!"
  Was my spirit's silent prayer,
While the shifting light and darkness
  Saw me standing lonely there;

Saw me standing, saw me waiting,
  In the awful shadow there,
Till, as clouds, my fears departing,
  Faded in the viewless air.

Then it was no longer doubting,
  That I sealed the happy choice;
And a coward tongue unloosing,
  Echoed then a fearless voice:

I will pass the golden portals
  And explore each secret part,
For I long to find a solace
  For my yearning, aching heart.

Then I issued from the darkness,
  I so long a plodding fool,
And the King in mercy led me
  Through the open vestibule;

And I passed the golden portals
  Which I ne'er had passed before,
Entered then the lofty chambers
  Where is love forever more.

And the music of low voices,
   Floating cheerily to me,
Added knowledge unto knowledge
   Touching immortality.

And I felt my spirit glowing,
   Joyous in its new-born power,
As a bud which in its blowing
   Feels itself at last a flower.

Lord, defend Thou me, Thy servant,
   With Thine everlasting grace,
Till I in Thy chambers yonder,
   Hail the brightness of Thy face.

Thine be all the praise and glory
   Which through Christ I bring to men!
Mine be but to tell His story,
   Till I breathe my last Amen!

The Beautiful Plant.

"The rose of Sharon and the lily of the valley."

Of all the wonderful plants that grow
  On mountain, in forest and field,
There are verily none of which I know
  Whose generous blossoms yield
One-half the fragrance, one-half so sweet,
As the Beautiful Plant that I daily meet.

It blooms the first in the vernal time,
  And gay at the coming of June;
It ever outlives the Summer's prime:
  And when the Autumn-winds tune
Their organs to play the dirge of death,
It scorneth and shunneth their blasting breath.

When Nature at length is in burial array,
  Her children all gone to the tomb,
Will it ever know that wickedest day
  When it shall be out of its bloom?
Oh, no; for every to-morrow doth bring
To my Beautiful Plant the return of Spring.

It drinketh the wine from the cup of morn,
  And trembles with rare delight;
And the loving stars at even born
  Look down from their homes of light,
And unto my heart forever say,
Thou hast the beauty that lives for aye.

And when I go forth to the strife of the world,
  And join the hurry and din,
With banners of light in my soul unfurled,
  I forget not that men are kin,
Throughout the one great household of God,
Awake on earth or asleep in the sod.

The present, the past, and the future are mine,
   And I am no longer my own:
All things I behold in the light divine,
   Where nothing is ever alone,
And beauty flows forth unto eager eyes
Surveying the earth or piercing the skies.

I cannot in isolation move,
   When I catch the glory of all
That is meant by Universal Love,
   To push from the heart the wall
Which is builded of hate and fear and doubt,
And fences immortal companions out.

My Beautiful Plant, athrough my heart
   Diffuses such glory and cheer,
I would never more from the garden depart
   Where it blossoms through all the year,
And daily, I think, becomes more fair,
Receiving the kisses of purer air.

Oh who does not nourish so holy a thing
  Is the poorest and vilest of all!
Though he live unchallenged a very king,
  And a world respond to his call.
Ah, such, I fear, when the earth is behind,
The garden immortal will never find;

For this plant is akin to the Tree of Life,
  Blossoming under its shade,
And serving to sweeten the toil and strife
  Which the Tempter for us has made,
Until at last we climb by its power
So high as to pluck the heavenly dower.

And then in truth of such wondrous worth,
  Its roots so deep in the soul,
That when we are weary and done with the earth,
  It will go with us over the goal;
And there at length in its native clime,
It will reach with its kindred a growth sublime.

EUREKA.

(For St. Andrew's Day, Nov. 30.)

"He first findeth his own brother Simon, and saith unto him, We have found the Messias."

St. Andrew and ten thousand others
Have told my secret to their brothers;
Yet there may be some little gain,
If now I tell it o'er again.

Though all my telling will not make
The hearer of the love partake,
Which is the sunshine of my story,
Its chief and everlasting glory.

It comes through strong, courageous years,
And hopes victorious over fears,
Through ceaseless toil by day and night,
Until the flashes of the light

Drive from the yearning soul afar
The things that of our selfhood are,
And fill its waiting chambers full
Of God, the one thing beautiful.

This secret of the world of spirit
God does not give for any merit
Which in His children He discovers.
He hails the truest of his lovers,

And unto them vouchsafes the grace
His truth eternal to embrace,
And clasp within an eager soul,
The secret which they aye control.

Eureka! cries Archimedes,
What time his secret fair he sees;
And forth he runs to publish it,
His face with glorious triumph lit.

Copernicus for many years.
Sought for the secret of the spheres:
Through forty circles of the earth
Was it in coming to its birth.

And when at last the old man died
At anchor in the Crucified,
The fruit of all his toil became
The glory of a deathless name.

Newton and Kepler both baptized
In prayer the truths which they so prized:
Thanksgiving unto God arose,
Who His arcana did disclose.

Oh, with what joy they told abroad
The long sought secrets of the Lord,
Apostles of science, Christian men,
Using the gifts of tongue and pen!

And shall the greater secret far
Than any truths of science are,
Remain a hidden, untold thing
With never wafting power of wing?

How did Saint Andrew finding Christ
The secret of his joy unpriced,
Straightway rehearse unto another,
Sharing his gladness with his brother!

How did Apostles tell it forth
Unto the East and West, the North
And South, wherever souls were found,
And clouds and darkness did abound!

Christ! Christ! did they alone rehearse,
The centre of the universe,
Round which humanity revolves,
What time it climbs in high resolves.

Christ! Christ! and Him once crucified,
Who for a world of sinners died.
Christ! Christ! who tasted death for all
Whom sin and evil here enthrall.

Henceforth all men to me are brothers.
I must tell Christ in me to others.
The fruit of all my long, long search
I must tell forth unto the Church.

And not the Church alone. The world
Must never see my banner furled.
One love, one work, until I die;
One only prize to fill mine eye.

O One exceeding great Reward!
Help me my secret tell abroad;
Help me one purpose to fulfill
What time on earth I do Thy will.

Through good report and evil I
Pursue whate'er in Christ is high,
And with the blessed Gospel shod
Range through the world-wide Church of God.

One only lofty vision I
Through all the earth and heavens descry:
One only fair ideal hold
Before my eager heart and bold.

One only song and prayer is mine
That I may show what is divine
Unto some yearning hearts of men
Groping for Paradise again.

And as the sovereign way for this
Return to paradisal bliss,
What is there, things of earth among,
Like breath of God upon the young?

Until they come at length to see
The beauty of the Deity,
Alike in Nature as in Grace,
Flashing from every form and place,

A guide to lead them on and on,
As love led the Apostle, John,
Till they begin to tell abroad
God, their exceeding great reward.

Dear Christ! all men to me are brothers.
Henceforth my secret is for others:
One only prize to hold mine eye,
One love, one work, until I die.

II.

Yes, I have found the work at last,
Which Providence alone forecast;
And nevermore for me in rest,
Save when I labor at my best.

Dear younger brother, wouldst thou know
The way the Master loves to show
His will and wish? The search is vain,
Unless it be through toil and pain.

There is no easy lesson here
Where wisdom lingers many a year.
Most their vocation never know,
Since wisdom comes so slow, so slow!

Discerning not the will of God,
They walk the way the fathers trod
And He who marks the sparrow's fall,
Observes his lowly children all.

But thou of hunger hast the smart
Pent up within a conscious heart.
God's providence is speaking there,
Telling what thou shouldst do and dare.

Be bold to heed the silent voice
And crucify each meaner choice;
Or else forever lose the place
Assigned thee in the realm of Grace

God speaks not many times to those
To whom His will He would disclose.
Have they, alas, no ears to hear,
No more, no more He draweth near.

He needs thee not against thy will.
Thy little place His hand can fill.
From stones can He, of old I AM,
Raise children unto Abraham.

So thou, thy work to know and do,
Must unto Providence be true,
And heed the signals and the signs,
Although the light but dimly shines.

What though the signs are not so plain
As to shut out all doubt and pain?
The doubt and pain will not grow less,
While thou remain'st in idleness.

What if the signals be but faint
And in thy heart there is complaint?
Ah, they will all the fainter be
During thine inactivity

When once the signal voice is heard,
And the unfathomed heart is stirred
To action, we have found the way
Where life is greater than to-day,

(However vast its treasures be)
And boldly claims eternity.
Henceforth we no more reckon worth
By the arithmetic of earth.

The great is small, the small is great,
Often in after estimate,
And nobler aims and visions rise
What time we see with other eyes

Hast thou despised the little things?
Know thou the smallest duty brings
A prophecy of coming time,
For thee ignoble or sublime.

The gifts of God thou dost not use,
Little or great, thou dost abuse
What if — the forfeit comes at last —
From thee be taken what thou hast?

Thy sacred trusts each day increase:
Evening shall bring a psalm of peace,
And in a broader circle shine
The lantern of the Word Divine.

The blessed things of God no more
Shall be like shadow, as before,
But real, precious and sublime,
To grow more fair by use and time

Stand still, the darkness on thy track
Pushes no more its column back.
Halt not, the light gleams wide and far,
And thine is an unsetting star.

There always will be clouds. Thy mark
May sometimes vanish in the dark.
What then? Wilt thou at this despair?
It is thy trial — oh, beware!

Renew thy faltering zeal and trust
The Lord, O creature of the dust.
Young faith will perish in the night,
If thou dost only walk by sight

Without the sun, the air, the earth,
The seed comes not unto its birth:
Its hidden power of life will die,
Or dormant in its prison lie.

Without the word and deed, the thought
Is to no blessed uses brought,
But quickly withers from the soul,
Evanishing beyond control.

Act to the purpose of thy heart,
And Providence, with wondrous art,
Shall fashion it to beauty there,
Transmuting all thy work and prayer,

Till it shall come to be thy life
Grown strong in every manly strife,
And, when the time is ripe, approve
Thee for the Master's work of love.

THE TRIUMPHAL ENTRY.

(GOSPEL FOR ADVENT SUNDAY. Tune, *New Jersey*, Number 433, Goodrich & Gilbert's Hymnal.)

Who is this in triumph riding,
  'Mid the branches of the palm,
While, on either side dividing,
  Lifts the throng their greeting psalm?

Prophet, Priest, and King and Saviour,
  He who left the throne on high,
Now, by His divine behavior,
  Drawing forth the people's cry.

He it is who comes in meekness,
  Though the Chief and Lord of all;
He it is who, strong in weakness,
  Frees His people from their thrall.

O my soul! go forth to meet Him
  Coming on His weary way;
Open wide thy gates and greet Him
  Sovereign of thy courts for aye.

The Eternal Song.

"And they sing the song of Moses, the servant of God, and the song of the Lamb, saying great and marvelous are thy works, Lord God Almighty; just and true are thy ways, thou King of saints."

Cometh soon the day desired long,
Cometh soon the triumph over wrong,
When we sing the one eternal song.

Lo! when heaven and earth shall both remove,
Cometh then Jerusalem above
Where the banner over all is love.

Oh the heights to which the saints shall climb!
Oh the wonders of that coming time,
Wonders for our telling too sublime!

Heaven and earth renewed, from crowns as bright
As is God's all-flaming, endless light,
Flash their beauty in the face of Night,

Till she from the universe away
Hastes to hide herself in that decay
Which shall have no resurrection day.

Soul! arise and see the splendor come!
For the painting of that fadeless home,
Voice and heart without the Lord are dumb.

John in Patmos saw the blessed sight,
An immortal and divine delight,
For unhallowed eyes too pure and bright,

New Jerusalem, a coming down,
City matchless in her far renown,
Bringing for each valiant saint a crown.

What is that great voice which followed then?
Lo! God's tabernacle is with men.
Former things shall be no more again;

THE ETERNAL SONG.

No more weeping — pain and death are done,
Who hath overcome hath all things won,
And shall ever be to God a son.

O my soul, hear thou that other voice,
And remember what hath been thy choice,
Ere thou lift a heart that may rejoice!

Lo! the fearful, unbelievers all,
Liars, they who down to idols fall,
Know the death whence there is no recall! —

Know the second death, which is the fire
Of a vanished season to aspire,
Burning, burning, in a vain desire.

Oh the terrors, when they vainly call
On the mountains and the rocks to fall
On them as annihilation's pall!

Help me, God, to shun that second death!
Help me while on earth I draw my breath!
Help me learn and do what Jesu. saith!

Hast thou chosen that eternal part,
Then at length is thine, O valiant heart,
Joy that shall not ever more depart.

Lift thine eyes and feast them on the grace,
Honor, riches in that radiant place,
Thine, when thou hast ended here thy race.

Get thee to a mountain great and high,
Get thee, O my soul, where best thine eye
Tracks the glory flaming down the sky.

City after an eternal plan;
City which the Lord's dear mercies span,
Bow, my heart, before this love to man!

Gates look North and South and East and West,
All unfolding what is fairest, best,
Light and truth and everlasting rest.

Jasper walls are there, and golden pave,
Of the sun and moon no need they have;
All the Lamb and God with glory lave.

THE ETERNAL SONG.

Hark! hark! hear that mighty rush of song,
From all souls that love has made so strong;
Hark, and learn the notes which they prolong!

Song of Moses and the Lamb they raise,
Pouring forth to God eternal praise,
Who is just and true in all His ways.

Moses and the Lamb with never taints!
Theirs the chant they lift without complaints:
Just and true Thy ways are, King of saints.

Moses! servant unto God below,
Mercies in His judgments thou did'st know,
Fountain whence eternal praises flow.

Lamb! who suffered'st here upon the cross,
And did'st purge away our sin and dross,
God in Thee did show the gain of loss.

Hear their voices who His Kingdom trod,
With the preparation of the Gospel shod:
Great and marvellous thy works, O God!

See them cast their crowns before the Throne,
Service which by them on earth was shown,
There at length unto perfection grown!

Looking back from new Jerusalem,
Know they with the Lord their diadem,
Tribulation was but love to them.

Oh the beauty love in mercy paints
When she chants the death of all complaints:
Just and true Thy ways are, King of saints!

Soul! arise and gird thine armor on.
Has the light of God within thee shone,
Linger not the rugged ways upon.

Thorns and crags and dangers, what are they
But prophetic of the fadeless bay,
Which the eager brow would wear for aye!

God through love shall make the mountains low;
God through love shall cause the depths to grow
Heights which everlasting sunshine know.

THE ETERNAL SONG.

Hast thou gained some triumph in the Lord,
Thinking more of coveted reward
Than of faithfulness unto His Word?

Hast thou ever drunk the cup of bitterness,
Flowing with the gall of deep distress,
When thou seemd'st to sink from less to less?

Tell me, thou with Christ within thy heart,
What thou thinkest of that olden smart,
And the triumph where thou hadst a part?

Rose I in my joy, and rising fell.
From my grief I rose too high to tell!
God be praised who doeth all things well.

Oh the beauty love in mercy paints,
When she chants the death of all complaints:
Just and true thy ways are, King of saints!

Girded in the armor of His light,
Take, my soul, thy rank amid the fight,
Counting on the triumph of the right.

What though clouds shall clasp thee in their bath?
What though night shall gloom along the path,
Where the Lord's the only guide one hath?

Fling thy splendor on the darkness here,
Till the ways of God becoming clear,
Banish from thy bosom every fear.

What though cruel things upon thee press,
Resting as a burden of distress,
Till thou cry, alas! for righteousness?

Recognize the long extended hand,
Moulding thee as for a purpose grand;
Fail not thou to do the Lord's command,

Knowing as thou lookest forth afar,
Life and death and all things glory are,
God's and His who flames the Morning Star.

Oh the beauty love in mercy paints,
When she chants the death of all complaints:
JUST AND TRUE THY WAYS ARE, KING OF SAINTS!

SIGNS.

(GOSPEL FOR SECOND SUNDAY IN ADVENT. Tunes, *Boylston*, or *Owen*,
page 73, Hymnal for Social and Public Worship.)

THE time is drawing nigh
  When He who came of old,
Shall leave again the courts on high,
  And visit here His fold.

And what if signs there be
  In all the world around,
That, calling to eternity,
  The trumpet soon will sound?

O comrade! look within,
  And see what signs are there,
What freedom from defiling sin,
  And for that day prepare.

And then, whate'er the watch
  In which the Lord appears,
His saving strength shall more than match
  A phantom host of fears.

ORDINATION HYMNS.

(For the Winter Ember Days. Tunes, *Benevolence* and *Hursley*, Numbers 437 and 336, Goodrich & Gilbert's Hymnal.)

I.

To those, O Lord, whom Thou dost call,
And set to watch on Zion's wall,
Give eagle eyes that they may see
All lurking foes of Thine and Thee;

Give words of power to warn Thy flock,
And save from every hostile shock;
Give strength to guard that heritage,
Which Thou hast loved from age to age.

Do Thou their shield and helmet be
In conflict with that enemy
Who works without, and works within,
To turn aside and lure to sin.

And while our prayers their hands uphold,
Bless Thou their work to Thy dear Fold,
Till eager throngs of sinners come
And find a refuge and a home.

II.

My Saviour, when I think of Thee,
And all Thou didst for love of me,
I cry for grace that I may know
How I Thy love may others show.

For this, O Lord, is mine to do,
And to my work I would be true,
To lead Thine erring ones to see
Thou lovest them as well as me.

Do Thou in this my efforts aid,
And with Thy love my soul pervade,
Until a guiding flame it burn
And wandering ones to Thee return.

Do Thou in this my labor bless,
And many unto righteousness
Shall I at length, O Lord, incline,
And as the stars forever shine.

THE DAY OF GOD.

(COLLECT FOR THIRD SUNDAY IN ADVENT. Tune, *Quaiffe*, not published.)

Are ye with the preparation
  Of the Gospel shod,
Fear ye not the tribulation
  Of the day of God!
He will come in all the glory
  Of a smiling face,
And rehearse the happy story
  Of a day of grace.

Are ye with no preparation
  Of the Gospel shod,
Then, alas! the tribulation
  Of the day of God!
He will come, but in the glory
  Of a frowning face,
And recall the fearful story
  Of His wasted grace.

ANGELS OF LIFE AND DEATH.

"Are they not all ministering spirits?"

OUR earth by two angels is trod,
Who bear the commissions of God,
All written in letters of light
To those who can read them aright.

One radiant, beautiful is,
Who comes with the message of bliss,
And sweet benediction to them
Who touch but his garments' bright hem.

He came when Elizabeth knew
The joy that so tenderly grew,
Until her reproach among men
Had passed to the things that had been:

When Mary, the Mother of One
Of Earth and of Heaven the Son,
Rejoiced in her God and her Saviour
With meek and with lowly behaviour.

We know his commission, and all
Are happier when his foot-fall
Is heard at the door of our mansion;
And greeting him, feel we expansion

Of joy that is blessed forever
What time it is crowned in endeavor
And tenderest love for the grace
That comes to our trembling embrace.

O beautiful angel! we know
Of nothing more pure than the glow
Of bosoms whose promises are
No longer, no longer afar.

No longer? The Angel of Life
Who quiets the bosom's first strife,
But wakens another far stronger
And fiercer and wilder and longer.

O father forecasting the joy
That dawns in a beautiful boy,
Until the far years of his prime
Are crowned with a manhood sublime!

O mother that dotest on one
As dear as the light of the sun,
And dreamest of him till his name
Is writ on the star-line of fame!

The rainbow so wondrously fair,
The painting of God in the air,
One moment entrances the eye,
The next, it is gone from the sky.

The flowers that spring at our feet,
All beautiful things that we meet,
Endure for an hour or a day
And yield to the touch of decay.

Alas and alas for the joy
That dawns in a beautiful boy,
Of all the dear joys of the breast
The purest and sweetest and best!

The radiant Angel of Light
May suddenly pass from the sight
And beckon the Angel of Gloom
To enter the dim, silent room;

Whose way is a way in the dark.
Oh, who can discover his mark?
For one shall be taken, one left;
One keepeth, and one is bereft.

Death comes at all seasons and places,
He stays not for fortune or graces:
His will is the will of the Lord.
Who would not submission accord?

Short joy is our heritage here;
With imperfect love there is fear,
Which troubles the stoutest heart long
With fitful and feverish song.

The bliss of a sweetness it knows,
The cup which with bitterness flows;
For Death is an Angel of Light,
Though robed in the garments of night,

Who comes for the young and the old,
To gather them all to the fold
Where greets the Good Shepherd His own,
And sorrow and tears are unknown.

All angels are angels of love.
Of God are both raven and dove:
One serveth the Ark in the Flood;
One bringeth the prophet his food.

All things of both heaven and earth
Are waiting an infinite birth.
The flush of a joy that has been,
Some day we shall know it again.

As yonder bright bow fades away,
As violets yield to decay,
And flowers yet again we may see,
And rainbows as fair there may be;

As day unto night must give way,
And night in its turns unto day,
Till dawns the perennial light
When there shall no longer be night;

So sorrow and joy — the two poles
Belonging on earth to all souls —
Until they are merged into one
When conflicts forever are done,

And saints all rejoice that they know
The better for trials the glow
Of bosoms whose promises are
No longer, no longer afar.

THE DOUBTERS' HYMN.

(For St. Thomas' Day. Tune, *Gower*, page 31, Greatorex Collection.)

Great Searcher of the troubled heart,
   We bow before Thy Throne
And pray Thee make our doubts depart,
   Till we are all Thine own.

Explore the chambers of our souls,
   Bring from the night the day,
Until, like clouds, the darkness rolls
   Forevermore away.

O Thou, in whom we trust, believe,
   Who are of sinners chief,
Our hearts' strong, wrestling prayer receive,
   And help our unbelief.

The blindness 'which for Thomas' sake,
   Thou didst of old remove,
From all our hearts in mercy take,
   And we our faith shall prove.

A Legend of St. Thomas.

Saint Thomas the day of his Festival,
  The briefest of the year,
Was looking down from Paradise
  Through the frosty air and clear.

His eye, the eye of heaven that morn,
  Was of worshipers in quest.
And traveled afar through all the North
  And South and East and West.

At length his ear he bended low,
  To catch the sounds that came
From a beautiful and lofty church
  Which bore his very name.

A LEGEND OF SAINT THOMAS.

It was no organ peal he heard.
   No voice of praise or prayer;
Nor was it the blessed Word of God
   Which rung through the arches there.

There was no low-bowed priest within,
   There was no reverence;
And the holy angels there had said
   "Arise, let us go hence."

The hearts of the angels who came to see
   What honor Saint Thomas had,
And gather the odors of prayer and praise,
   Were heavy, that day, and sad.

They only beheld a noisy throng
   Who were binding wreaths to grace
The house of God for Christmas-tide,
   At a sacred time and place:

As if they honored the Holy Child
   By what was another's loss!
As if it absolved from irreverence,
   The making of garland and cross!

Then quickly the Saint from Paradise
  Came down the wintry sky,
And his form which in the window stood
  Was a glory to every eye.

His face was a heavenly beauty there
  Of which the artist dreamed,
That never before until that day
  Had more than mortal seemed.

The gazers ceased their nimble work,
  The hum of voices died;
All wondered what was shining there
  Which the place so glorified.

And more and more the wonder grew
  Until Saint Thomas saw
Fast creeping on from face to face
  A shadow of breathless awe.

They knew not the Saint was looking in
  Through the beautiful window there;
But something whispered from heart to heart,
  "My house is a house of prayer."

And something guided many a hand
  Until from the church they bore
All that unhallowed the sacred place,
  And order reigned once more.

And lo! the angels all came back,
  And their hearts at length were glad,
When they gathered the odors of prayer and saw
  What honor Saint Thomas had.

Epithalamium.

"Thy lips, O my spouse, drop honey as the honey-comb."

(Tune, *Wir Pflugen*, page 102.)

What time I send my greeting,
O friends to me so dear,
And pray your happy nuptials
May gladden many a year;

What time I see the honey
So sweet upon the lips,
My heart—I cannot hold it—
Into the future dips.

I see the Bride and Bridegroom,
My yearning soul before,
To me a calling, calling;
I cannot linger more.

It is the Great Espousal
To last forevermore,
The joy we have a taste of
Upon this earthly shore.

It is the Marriage Supper;
The Bridegroom and the Bride,
Within the waiting mansions
Are standing side by side.

He is the King of Glory,
He is the Prince of Peace;
His triumphs are recorded,
The joy shall never cease.

He stands as one victorious,
And looketh on the Bride,
Who there is all as glorious
A standing by his side.

The daughter she of Zion,
Who here was dark and low:
When lifted by the Lion,
What beauty did she show?

The garments of His beauty,
She wore through all the earth,
And showed to all her children
The splendor of His worth.

Her lips they dropped with honey,
Her garments smelt of myrrh;
Better than wine or money
The love He showed to her.

What time I see the honey
So sweet upon the lips,
My heart—I cannot hold it—
Into the future dips.

It is the Marriage Supper;
The Bridegroom and the Bride,
Within the Father's mansions
Are standing side by side.

Long since the invitations
Went forth through all the world,
And flashed from off the banners
Which never here are furled.

The children of the Kingdom
Are coming from afar;
From Greece and Rome and England,
Wherever altars are.

And Wesley's lowly chapel
Is not without its roll;
Geneva comes and yieldeth
The fruit of many a soul.

I see among them Luther
Full many a column bring;
An everlasting castle
Ist unser Gott, they sing.

Jerusalem, the olden,
Sends many children there:
Jerusalem, the Golden,
Receiveth all the fair.

They seek the Father's mansions,
A great unnumbered throng,
Who in their tribulation
Have trampled sin and wrong.

THE YEAR OF CHRIST.

The Bride and Bridegroom greet them;
They are the chosen guests,
The children of the Kingdom,
Who did the Lord's behests.

They greet the Bride and Bridegroom;
Both His and hers they are,
The fruit of all her travail,
Her children from afar.

Their lips they drop with honey,
Their garments smell of myrrh;
Better than wine or money,
The love from Him and her.

The Bridegroom looketh over
The blessed throng so vast;
His eye, the jealous Lover's,
Upon them all is cast.

What time each face He greeteth,
As one to Him well known,
He sees they all to whiteness
And purity have grown.

His blood alone redeemed them,
And made them pure and fair:
His righteousness still clothes them,
They yet receive His care.

But hark! a cry ariseth,
That does not all rejoice.
Oh, hark! a voice ascendeth,
It is the Bridegroom's voice:

"O children of the Kingdom
Why are ye not all here?
Where are unnumbered faces
That were to me so dear?"

It is the cry that ranges
Through all the Universe,
The cry that never changes—
Who can its woe rehearse?

"O children of the Kingdom,
Who did in darkness stay,
There is an outer darkness
That doth not roll away."

"O children of the Kingdom,
Who wallowed in the mire,
There is a Day Eternal,
There is a quenchless fire."

"O children of the Kingdom,
Who did not My command,
Ye cannot in My presence
Like these, in gladness stand."

"O children of the Kingdom,
To whom My love was shown,
Your souls are full of darkness,
Ye only have your own."

God! God! The gall that drippeth,
So bitter to my taste,
What time I feel their blindness,
Who grace so precious waste!

The cry! the cry that ranges
Through all the Universe,
The cry that never changes—
Who can its woe rehearse?

"O children of the Kingdom,
To whom God's love was shown,
Your souls are filled with darkness,
Ye only have your own!"

I turn and see the mansions,
The Father's House within,
The guests, the Bride, and Bridegroom,
Who washed away their sin.

He is the King of Glory,
He is the Prince of Peace;
His triumphs are God's story,
The joy shall never cease.

He stands as one victorious,
And looketh on the Bride,
Who there is all as glorious,
A standing by His side.

What time I see the honey
So sweet upon the lips,
My heart—I cannot hold it—
Into the future dips.

While children of the Kingdom,
Without in darkness grope,
I see them coming, coming!
All in the blessed hope;

From out the East a coming,
The land of far renown;
From out the West a coming,
And bearing many a crown;

From out the North a coming,
From wild barbarian lands;
From out the South a coming,
Where Sheba's queen commands;

They seek the Father's mansions,
Where Abraham is found
With Isaac too and Jacob,
Where joys untold abound.

Behold the Bride and Bridegroom
Are standing at the door,
And give them all the greeting
Of love forevermore.

Their lips they drop with honey,
Their garments smell of myrrh;
Better than wine or money,
The love from Him and her.

And who is he that standeth,
Clothed in immortal youth?
Is it the one who taught me
To climb in search of truth?

And who is this who gazeth
The myriad throng upon?
Is it the one whose thunder
Reached him of Macedon?

And who is this that looketh
With such abounding peace?
Is it old Cincinnatus
Whose rest shall never cease?

I cannot count the faces
Which glow with olden grace.
Perhaps, when earth shall vanish,
With them will be my place.

The children of the Kingdom
And aliens are there:
Jerusalem, the Golden,
Receiveth all the fair.

The wedding now is furnished,
The Marriage Supper come;
And there is song aud feasting
In that Eternal Home.

Behold the Great Espousal
To last forevermore,
The joy we have a taste of
Upon this earthly shore.

He is the King of Glory,
He is the Prince of Peace;
The Daughter she of Zion,
The joy shall never cease.

He stands as one victorious
And looketh on the Bride,
Who there is all as glorious,
A standing by His side.

The Lamb is life and glory,
The Church is at her rest,
An everlasting service,
The fairest and the best.

As heart to heart then answers,
In Bridegroom and the Bride,
So all are one forever
And with the Lord abide.

ADVENT LONGING.

(FIRST EVENING LESSON, FOURTH SUNDAY IN ADVENT. Tune, *Sweet Home* without the chorus.)

Who, who does not yearn for the Kingdom of God,
The realm which the wise of all ages have trod,
When striving with sin and combatting with sense,
Jehovah the helmet and shield of defense.

O, who does not yearn for the Kingdom of God,
The realm which the meek of all ages have trod,
Where Christ, the Good Shepherd, so true to His charge,
Keeps watch on the weary, their strength to enlarge.

O, who does not yearn for the Kingdom of God,
The realm where the brave of all ages have trod,
And labored in faith, and been victors in love
Through the might of their heirship to glory above.

Who, who does not yearn for the Kingdom of God,
The realm which the Saints of all ages have trod,
Who now in their triumph are crowned with their Lord,
And rest in the truth of His glorious Word.

THE NATIVITY.

I.

O SHEPHERDS watching flocks by night,
How bursts upon your startled sight,
The glory of the heavenly light!

Ye see the splendor of the sky
Down streaming into mortal eye,
And every heart doth wonder why.

But hark! what voice is that ye hear,
Than mortal accents far more clear,
Like strange, sweet music to the ear?

Fear not! It is an angel's voice:
He speaks to make the world rejoice,
And ye of heralds are his choice.

Good tidings of great joy brings he,
Which shall unto all people be
Till they from sin and death be free;

For unto you this winter morn
A Saviour, Christ, the Lord, is born,
Who Satan of his realm hath shorn.

And Bethlehem doth now behold
The Babe the prophets saw of old
Before the ages were unrolled.

II.

O all ye angels, worship Him!
O ever flaming Cherubim,
Bow low! and ye, O Seraphim.

The time that Wisdom chose is come,
When joy gives voice to even the dumb,
And Jesu leaves the Father's home.

The season long desired is ripe,
Foretold in prophecy and type,
And from all eyes the tears to wipe

He comes. Lo! Angels throng the sky
Where voice to voice doth make reply,
"Be glory now to God on high."

And dear words than tongue or pen
May ever speak or write again,
"Peace! peace on earth, good will to men."

III.

As soon as e'er the sky is grey
With tokens of the coming day,
The wondering shepherds go their way

In silence and with one accord,
To seek their Saviour and their Lord,
According to the Angel's word.

Behold, all in the lowly place
They find the more than mortal Grace
And look upon His radiant face.

The tribute of meek hearts they bring,
The first to fall a worshipping
In presence of the new-born King.

And finding such divine reward,
The wonder of the infant Lord
They carry hence and spread abroad.

IV.

O hearts that beat in latter days
And lift no voice of prayer or praise,
Heed ye what now God's angel says.

He bringeth every lowly heart
Good tidings of the better part.
Oh, straightway from your sins depart!

Approach, approach the Saviour's shrine
Where more than mortal glories shine,
And henceforth know the light divine.

And when your grateful souls are full
Of all that is most beautiful,
How quick will they grow dutiful,

And in among the ranks of men
In burning words of tongue or pen,
Sow all their harvest store again!

The Christmas Service,

with infant baptism.

I.

PROCESSIONAL.

(Tune, *Tabor*, No. 339, Goodrich & Gilbert's Hymnal.)

The banners of light are unfurled,
  The darkness is sovereign no more,
And tidings of joy to the world
  Are speeding from shore unto shore.

For Bethlehem's plains have beheld
  A wonderful, beautiful sight,
Which prophets foreshadowed of eld,
  A new and immortal delight.

Divinity clothed in the flesh
  Now hallows the long waiting earth,
And nations, all starting afresh,
  Shall go on from worth unto worth.

The Babe in a manger is laid,
  For such was the cradle, dear Lord,
And shepherds, their charge now obeyed,
  Are spreading their wonder abroad.

O spread it abroad till the day
  The Christ shall be born in all hearts,
And humility rise to the sway
  Where pride with its folly departs.

II.

THE SERVICE.

The greeting processional song,
By voices of youth borne along,

Flowed chancel and transept and nave
All through with its musical wave:

When lo, from his place in the east
Was heard the clear voice of the priest,

With humble confession from all,
The low-kneeling penitents' call;

And then abso'ution and prayer
Were borne by His messengers there,

THE CHRISTMAS SERVICE.

The angels who wait on His word,
Above to the answering Lord.

The wonderful Psalms for the day
Divinity took our array;

The Prophet forecasting the time,
All glowing with vision sublime:

Te Deum Laudamus, which bears
The incense of praises and prayers:

Saint Luke, as with magical pen,
Describing the advent to men

Of Him the dear Saviour of all,
Who came as at mercy's meek call;

All these in their order were heard,
And was there a bosom not stirred?—

A heart of the young or the hoary,
Not lighted anew with the glory

That shone on that wonderful day
Divinity stooped to array

Itself in humanity's dress,
Our nature forever to bless?

And now in the hush and the pause
That followed the thought of the Cause

Of tidings of joy to the world,
Whose banners of light are unfurled,

One under those banners was made
A soldier of Christ, and arrayed

In armor divine for the strife
And all the temptations of life.

The baptismal water was there
All hallowed and blest as by prayer,

Through him the meek priest of the Lord,
Appointed as erst by His word,

And poured on our infant's fair brow,
What time were the promise and vow

Of parents and sponsors received
On high, as of those who believed,

Rejoicing that merciful Heaven
Had promises lovingly given

To them and their children and all
Far off whom the Saviour should call.

O Christ! 'twas a beautiful sight,
And more than a mortal delight,

The seeing one brought to Thy fold,
And under Thy banner enrolled,

A child of the Lord on the morn
That Thou of a Virgin wast born!

Now grand was the service in store,
Companion of what went before:

The out-burst of blessing and praise
Which many a heart did upraise;

The naming of faith we all hold,
Delivered to Saints once of old;

The blessed communion of prayer
Ascending through angel-thronged air

THE YEAR OF CHRIST.

To Him who omnipotent there
Doth heed what our litanies bear;

A sweet song of David who sung
As if to a harp that was strung

By angels, and then (to prelude
The feast of the Body and Blood

All broken and poured out for thee,
The chiefest of sinners like me)

The tables, which given of old,
Have brightened with years that have rolled;

The Collect for daily renewal
Of natures which sin has made dual;

Epistle and Gospel which raise
The thoughts to the Ancient of Days;

A song of rejoicing once more
Which reverent voices upbore;

Meek words of salvation which came
From lips that were touched as by flame

From Christ's dear altar of love;
And then, last of all, all above

In joyful, glorious might,
The Eucharist-feast of delight!

Oh, such was the service that day
Divinity took our array,

While angels of praise and of prayer
Did hover more lovingly there,

Because of that dear little child
Not yet by temptation beguiled,

That, set in the midst, was a type
For those who in years were more ripe.

With such aspirations abounding,
Was not it a fitting surrounding

For that consecration to One,
As then, born a pure Virgin's Son

Who dowered, that glorious time,
A child for a mission sublime?

III.

RECESSIONAL.

(Tune, For thee, O dear, dear Country, No. 492, Goodrich & Gilbert's Hymnal.)

O Christ! the Child forever,
   Receive our child-like song;
For we Thy praises never
   Would cease to bear along
Through fair or stormy weather,
   Where'er our path may be,
Till Thou at length shall gather
   Thy little ones to Thee.

O Christ! the Man forever,
   Receive our humble prayer,
And crown our strong endeavor
   To cast aside despair,
And work as Thou desirest
   In love of Thee and Thine,
Till Thou our all requirest
   Before the upper shrine.

O Christ! the Priest forever,
  Receive our sacrifice,
Its good from evil sever
  And bear it to the skies;
Through trials and temptation,
  O bring us in Thy love,
And keep us for the nation
  Of all the blest above.

O Christ! our God forever,
  We all Thy word embrace,
And as by faith's strong lever,
  Would rise from grace to grace;
Rain Thou on us Thy manna,
  What time we here remain,
And ours shall be, Hosanna,
  When Thou shalt come again.

THE YEAR OF CHRIST.

Music by L. H. THOMAS.

Have ye no carol for the Lord, To spread His love, His love abroad? Have ye no carol for the Lord, To spread, His love, His love abroad?

CHORUS.

A Christmas Carol.

I.

This is the winter morn,
  Our Saviour, Christ, was born,
Who left the realms of endless day,
  To take our sins away.
Have ye no Carol for the Lord,
  To spread His love abroad?
Hosanna! from all our hearts we raise,
  Hosanna! Hosanna!
And make our lives His praise.

II.

Ring, ring, O happy bells!
  A blessed angel tells
The story of His humble birth,
  Who came this day to earth.
Have ye no praises for the Lord
  To spread His love abroad?
Hosanna! from all our hearts we pour,
  Hosanna! Hosanna!
And bless Him evermore.

III.

The shepherds vigils keep
  And watch by night their sheep:
Upon the plains of Bethlehem
  What glory comes to them!
Have ye from heaven no glory felt,
  Who all in prayer have knelt?
Hosanna! in all our hearts is light,
  Hosanna! Hosanna!
God's worship is delight.

IV.

A clear, angelic voice,
  To make the world rejoice,
Brings men good tidings of great joy,
  Which shall all hearts employ.
Have ye no precious word to bear,
  To make the world more fair?
Hosanna! from all our hearts shall flow,
  Hosanna! Hosanna!
Where'er on earth we go.

V.

The trembling shepherds hear,
  An angel calms their fear;
Lo! Christ in swaddling bands arrayed,
  Is in a manger laid.

Have ye no word of great delight,
  To bring the day from night?
Hosanna! in all our hearts shall be,
  Hosanna! Hosanna!
Through all eternity.

VI.

All in the lowly place
  They find the Royal Grace,
And lo! they fall a worshipping
  Before the new-born King.
Have ye no worship for the Lord,
  To give with one accord?
Hosanna! in all our hearts we bring,
  Hosanna! Hosanna!
Our lives our offering.

VII.

Their grateful hearts are full
  Of things most beautiful;
And lo! the wonder of the Lord
  They straightway spread abroad.
Have ye no beauty of the Christ
  Whose love has long sufficed?
Hosanna! from all our hearts we raise,
  Hosanna! Hosanna!
And carry hence His praise.

THE DEATH OF ST. STEPHEN.

(*Wir Pflugen*, the music for this Carol, was found by Mr. THOMAS in an old English Hymnal, copies of which are very rare. Except in the "Hymnal for Social and Public Worship," compiled by himself, he is not aware of its use in this country.)

I.

PRAISE GOD for that dear Martyr,
  The first of all the host
Who earth for heaven barter,
  To love the Master most;
And chief of sons and daughters
  Triumphant over pain,
Who cast upon the waters
  The bread that comes again.

II.

The nearest to the Saviour
  Who poured His blood for all,
And like Him in behaviour,
  We keep his festival,
In love of His devotion
  To Him who went before,
Through Whom we seek the portion
  For all the saints in store.

III.

We all in joy remember
  The valor of his life,
Which kindling every ember,
  Gives ardor to the strife,
In which of old the Master
  Dropped victory on one

Who through the world's disaster
Now shineth as the sun.

IV.

There was not one divining,
  When Stephen's face so fair
Was like an angel's shining,
  Whom he saw standing there
In that high place of glory,
  All at the Father's side,
Above heroic story,
  In that for foes he died.

V.

O strong young man, and burning
  For slaughter of the saints,
To that brave martyr turning
  Thou didst not hear complaints;
But grace to him way given
  To gain thy pardon there,
What time he went to heaven
  Upon the wings of prayer.

VI.

O Paul once filled with loathing
  At that bold Nazarene,
When at thy feet his clothing
  Was laid, what did that mean?—

But that on thee his spirit
  Would like a mantle fall,
Who through the Saviour's merit
  Wast soon the chief of all?

VII.

The saint is yet a mountain
  Against the wrath of foes.
His heart is still a fountain
  From whence devotion flows.
His blood has many a harvest
  In all the ages brought.
O foolish one that starvest,
  He did not live for nought.

VIII.

Thank God for that dear Martyr,
  The first of all the host
Who earth for heaven barter,
  To love the Saviour most;
And chief of sons and daughters
  Triumphant over pain,
Who cast upon the waters
  The bread that comes again.

A Legend of St. John.

(For his Festival, Dec. 27.)

There is a beautiful legend
  Come down from ancient time,
Of John, the beloved disciple,
  With the marks of his life sublime.

Eusebius has the story
  On his quaint, suggestive page;
And God in the hearts of His people
  Has preserved it from age to age.

It was after the vision in Patmos,
  After the sanctified love
Which flowed to the Seven Churches,
  Glowing with light from above:

When his years had outrun the measure
  Allotted to men at the best,
And Peter and James and the others
  Had followed the Master to rest:

At Ephesus came a message
  Where he was still at his post,
Which unto the aged Apostle
  Was the voice of the Holy Ghost.

Into the country he hastened
  With all the ardor of youth,
Shod with the preparation
  Of the Gospel of peace and truth.

His mission was one of mercy
  To the sheep that were scattered abroad,
And abundant consolation,
  Which flowed through him from the Lord.

Oh, would my art could paint him,
  The venerable man of God,
So lovingly showing and treading
  The way the Master had trod.

At length when the service was ended
  His eye on a young man fell,
Of beautiful form and feature
  And grace we love so well.

At once he turned to the bishop,
   And said with a love unpriced,
"To thee, to thee I commit him
   Before the Church and Christ."

He then returned to the city,
   The beloved disciple, John,
Where the strong unceasing current
   Of his deathless love flowed on.

The bishop discharged his duty
   To the youth so graceful and fair;
With restraining hand he held him,
   And trained him with loving care.

At last, when his preparation
   Was made for the holy rite,
He was cleansed in the sanctified water
   And pronounced a child of light.

For a time he adorned the doctrine
   Which Christ in the Church has set.
But, alas, for a passionate nature
   When Satan has spread his net!

Through comrades base and abandoned
  He was lured from day to day,
Until, like a steed unbridled,
  He struck from the rightful way:

And a wild, consuming passion
  Raised him unto the head
Of a mighty band of robbers,
  Of all the country the dread.

Time passed. Again a message
  Unto the Apostle was sent,
To set their affairs in order
  And tell them the Lord's intent.

And when he had come and attended
  To all that needed his care,
He turned him and said, "Come, Bishop,
  Give back my deposit so rare."

"What deposit?" was the answer
  Which could not confusion hide.
"I demand the soul of a brother,"
  Plainly the Apostle replied,

"Which Christ and I committed
   Before the Church to thee."
Trembling and even weeping,
   "The young man is dead," groaned he.

"How dead? what death" John demanded.
   "He the way of the tempter trod,
Forgetting the Master's weapon,
   And now he is dead unto God.

Yonder he roves a robber."
   "A fine keeper," said John, " indeed
Of a brother's soul. Get ready
   A guide and a saddled steed."

And all as he was an Apostle
   Into the region rode
Where the robber youth and captain
   Had fixed his strong abode.

When hardly over the border,
   He a prisoner was made,
And into their leader's presence,
   Demanded to be conveyed.

And he who could brave a thousand
  When each was an enemy,
Beholding John approaching,
  Turned him in shame to flee.

But John of his age forgetful,
  Pursued him with all his might.
"Why from thy defenceless father"
  He cried, "dost thou turn in flight?"

"Fear not: there is hope and a refuge,
  And life shall yet be thine.
I will intercede with the Master
  And task His love divine."

Subdued by love that is stronger
  Than was ever an armed band,
He became once more to the Father
  A child to feel for His hand.

Subdued by love that is stronger
  Than a world full of terrors and fears,
He returned to the House of the Father
  Athrough the baptism of tears.

Such is the beautiful legend,
  Come down from ancient days,
Of love that is young forever,
  And is he not blind who says,

That charity ever faileth,
  Or doth for a moment despair,
Or that there is any danger
  Too great for her to dare;

When John, the beloved disciple,
  With the faith of the Gospel shod,
Went forth in pursuit of the robber
  And brought him back to God?

The Holy Innocents.

December 28.

" Rachel, weeping for her children and would not be comforted, because they were not"

I have heard the voice in Ramah,
  And with sorrow we are not done;
For thine is the bitterest mourning,
  Mourning for an only son!

And what shall I utter to comfort
  The heart that is dearest of all?
Too young for the losses and crosses?
  Too young for the rise and the fall?

Oh, yes; we own it, we own it;
  But not too young for the grace
That was so nameless and blameless,
  For the yearning and tender embrace!

He hung, he hung on thy bosom
  In that happiest weariest hour,
A dear little bird to its blossom,
  The beautiful dutiful flower.

And thus he grew by its sweetness,
  He grew by its sweetness so
That smile unto smile responded—
  But a little while ago!

And you—and I?—were happy
  In many a vision fair
Of a ripe and glorious manhood
  Which the world and we should share.

In a little while the patter
  Of two little feet was heard;
And many a look it cheered us,
  A look that was more than a word.

In a little while he uttered
  The words we longed to hear;
And mama and papa blessed him
  With a blessing of hope and fear.

In a little while he budded,
 A bud of the promising spring,
And oh for the beautiful blossom,
 And oh for the fruit it will bring!

Oh the joy they never may know it
 Who never have parents been,
The joy of a swelling bosom
 With a growing light within:

A light that is soft and tender
 And growing in strength and grace,
Which wreathes a form that is slender
 And glows in a dear little face!

But life it knoweth the shadow,
 The shadow as well as the shine;
For the one it follows the other,
 And both together are thine

For the bud it never unfolded,
 The light it flickered away,
And whose is the power to utter
 The grief of that bitterest day?

His form is yet before me
　With the fair and lofty brow,
And the day since last we kissed it—
　Is it long since then and now?

Dearest, it seems but a minute,
　Though winter has twice spread the snow,
Meek purity's mantle to cover
　The one that is resting below.

In the acre of God that is yonder
　And unto the west his head,
He sleepeth the sleep untroubled,
　With one to watch at his bed.

For the bright and guardian angel
　Who beholdeth the Father's face,
Doth stand as a sentinel watching
　O'er the dear one's resting place;

Doth stand as a sentinel guarding
　The dust of the precious dead,
Till at length the trumpet soundeth
　When the years of the world are sped;

And the throng which cannot be numbered
  Put on their garments of white,
And gird themselves for the glory
  Of a realm that hath no night.

And so is gone, the darling,
  And the dream so fair and vain,
Whose light has faded to darkness,
  We shall never dream again!

Never? Is the earth the limit
  To bright and beautiful hope?
If the world brings not fruition,
  Must we in darkness grope?

Oh no! There is expectation
  Which the grave cannot control;
There is boundless infinite promise
  For the living and deathless soul.

And the darling who left us early,
  May yonder grow a man;
And in deeds of the great Hereafter
  May take his place in the van.

Oh, if thine is the bitterest mourning,
   Mourning for an only son,
Believe that in God, the Giver,
   Thy darling his course begun;

Believe that in God, the Taker,
   His course forever will be;
For this is the blessed comfort,
   The comfort for thee and me.

ECCLESIA.

(For the Sunday after Christmas.)

"Behold the handmaid of the Lord."

My place is among the lilies,
   Where He my beloved feeds;
I seek only where His will is,
   To satisfy all my needs.

His purity is the garment
   Which only I wish to wear;
A Bride for the Morning Star meant,
   I seek to be pure and fair.

I wonder, with all the order
   Of Him who doth yonder stand,
He looketh on my disorder
   And leadeth me by the hand,

What time I desire the splendor
　　Which glows in His blessed face,
And seek unto Him to render
　　A service for all His grace!

Oh have ye not known a lover
　　With tenderest care aglow,
What I in my love discover
　　Ye certainly cannot know.

With love and with beauty laden,
　　All which unto Him I owe,
I am in His sight a maiden
　　Wherever on earth I go.

But when at the last in Heaven
　　I stand at the Bridegroom's side,
To me will the joy be given,
　　Forever to be His Bride.

Engagement Song.

Remember that happiest day
When I from myself turned away,
And sought my devotion to prove
In acts of adorable love?

Oh, yes; I remember it well;
How could I forget it, the spell
That lifted me up from my fall,
And sang in my bosom the call,

To enter the long whitened field
That harvests for heaven doth yield,
And bind up the bright golden sheaves
Which God to a coronet weaves?

O fairest of all to my heart,
My love for thee will not depart,
Till yonder in bowing me down,
I cast at the foot-stool my crown.

THE MARRIAGE GARMENT.

FOR THE FIRST SUNDAY IN THE MONTH.

(Tune, *Humility*, Oliver Collection.)

THE marriage garment God requires,
   Is one I cannot all describe:
It is the heart with true desires
   That will not take the Tempter's bribe;

It is the thought of all we are,
   The wrestling prayer that sin may be
To-morrow less a frowning bar
   Between us and His purity;

It is the heart that doth forgive
   Whate'er our brother meant for ill,
The wish as in God's sight to live
   And evermore to do His will;

It is the strong and far resolve
  Which flames the toil of each to-day,
The hopes that higher still revolve
  What time the seasons pass away;

It is the love which reaches men
  Whatever be their place of birth,
The deed that seeks to make again
  A very paradise of earth.

Do I the marriage garment wear,
  And seek, O Lord, through Thy control,
That this vile heart may grow more fair,
  The Bread and Wine shall feast my soul.

THE TRAVELER.

For the Circumcision and New Year Day.

Oh did you not see him that over the snow
Came on with a pace so cautious and slow? —

That measured his step to a pendulum-tick
Arriving in town when the darkness was thick?

I saw him last night with locks so gray
A little way off as the light died away.

And I knew him at once so often before
Had he silently, mournfully passed at my door.

He must be cold and weary, I said,
Coming so far with that measured tread.

I will urge him to linger awhile with me
Till his withering chill and weariness flee.

A story—who knows?—he may deign to rehearse,
And when he is gone I will put it in verse.

I turned to prepare for the coming guest,
With curious troublous thoughts oppressed.

The window I cheered with the taper's glow
Which glimmered afar o'er the spectral snow.

My anxious care the hearth-stone knew
And the red flames leaped and beckoned anew.

But chiefly myself with singular care
Did I for the hoary presence prepare.

Yet with little success as I paced the room
Did I labor to banish a sense of gloom

My thoughts were going and coming like bees,
With store from the year's wide-stretching leas,

Some laden with honey, some laden with gall,
And into my heart they dropped it all!

O miserable heart! at once overrun
With the honey and gall thou can'st not shun.

O wretched heart! in sadness I cried,
Where is thy trust in the Crucified?

And in wrestling prayer did I labor long
That the Mighty One would make me strong.

That prayer was more than a useless breath:
It brought to my soul God's saving health.

When the hours went by on their sluggish flight,
And came the middle watch of the night;

In part unmanned in spite of my care,
I beheld my guest in the taper's glare,

A wall of darkness around him thick,
As onward he came to a pendulum-tick.

Then quickly I opened wide the door
And bade him pass my threshold o'er,

And linger awhile away from the cold,
And repeat some story or ballad old, —

His weary limbs to strengthen with rest,
For his course to the ever receding west.

THE TRAVELER.

Through the vacant door in wonder I glanced
And stood—was it long?—as one entranced.

Silence so aweful did fill the room
That tick of the clock was a cannon's boom.

And my heart it sank to its lowest retreat
And in whelming awe did muffle its beat.

For now I beheld as never before
And heard to forget, ah, nevermore!

For with outstretched hand, with sythe glass,
With naught of a pause did the traveler pass.

And with upturned face he the silence broke
And thus as be went he measur'dly spoke:

My journey is long, but my limbs are strong:
And I stay not for rest, for story, or song.

It is only a dirge, that ever I sing;
It is only of death the tale that I bring:

Of death that is life as it cometh to pass;
Of death that is death, alas! alas!

And these I chant as I go on my way,
As I go on my way forever and aye.

Call not thyself wretched, though bitter and sweet
In thy cup at this hour intermingle and meet.

Some cloud with the sunshine must ever appear,
And darkness prevails till morning is near.

But who doth remember the gloom of the night,
When the sky is aglow with the beautiful light?

Oh alas! if thou drinkest the bitter alone,
Nor heaven nor earth may stifle thy moan!

Thy moan!— and the echo died away,
Thy moan! thy moan forever and aye!

His measured voice I heard no more,
But not till I stand on eternity's shore,

And the things of time be forgotten all,
Shall I cease that traveler's words to recall.

As onward he moved to a pendulum-tick
The gloom and the darkness around him thick,

I fell on my knees and breathed a prayer;
And it rose I ween through the midnight air

To a God who knoweth the wants and all
The evil and good of this earthly thrall:

To One who suffered as on this day
And began our sins to purge away:

To Him who hath promised to heed our cry
And a troubled heart to purify.

And I feel that the gall will ever grow less
Till I see His face in righteousness.

And now my soul is filled with cheer
For the march of a bright and Happy New Year.

As years roll on, whether sun doth shine
Or clouds overcast, I will never repine;

For I know, when the race of time is run
I shall enter a realm of Eternal Sun.

NEW YEAR DAY.

Tune, *Anonymous*, as und.r.)

NEW YEAR DAY.

Year by year the world grows older,
  Year by year the end draws nigh.
Will the hearts of men be colder
  When the Lord descends the sky?
Soon the days will fill their number,
  Soon be here the time for rest;
Rouse ye, rouse ye from your slumber,
  Do the work that is the best:

Chorus.   Ever as with meek behaviour,
        Looking for the Lord and Saviour,
        In the brightness of His favour
          Finding Him reward and rest.

Year by year the day approaches
  When the Saviour will return.
See ye that no sin encroaches,
  Ye that for His coming yearn.
Have ye aught to do for neighbor,
  Do it ere the time for rest;
Going forth to toil and labor,
  Do the work that is the best:

        Chorus.

Help ye, help ye, one another,
   If ye seek the Golden Year;
Greet in every man a brother,
   Oh, how soon will it be here!
Journeying a little longer,
   Doing that which is the best,
We shall all be growing stronger
   Till we enter into rest:

     CHORUS.

What! and will ye idly linger
   In this strange and hostile land?
At the road side see the Finger
   Pointing to the Golden Strand
Rich in all eternal treasures,
   Purest, fairest, and the best,
Radiant with those endless pleasures
   Which are joy, reward and rest:

     CHORUS.

www.ingramcontent.com/pod-product-compliance
Lightning Source LLC
Chambersburg PA
CBHW020106170426
43199CB00009B/421